TIM DUNCAN

Slam Duncan

by

Kevin Kernan

SPORTS PUBLISHING INC.
www.SportsPublishingInc.com

Series editor: Rob Rains
Production manager: Susan M. McKinney
Production Coordinator: Erin J. Sands
Cover design: Scot Muncaster/Todd Lauer
Photo editor: Terrence C. Miltner
Photos: AP/Wide World Photos

ISBN: 1-58261-179-3
Library of Congress Catalog Card Number: 99-68597

SPORTS PUBLISHING INC.
SportsPublishingInc.com

Printed in the United States.

Contents

Tim, right, holds his NBA Finals MVP trophy while David Robinson shows off his first championship trophy. (AP/Wide World Photos)

1

The Man Behind the Camera

Here he was, seven feet tall and on top of the basketball world. With all eyes on him, Tim Duncan decided to look back. At 23, he knew this was the time of his young life and he wanted to enjoy it in his own way.

In a few moments the MVP Trophy would soon be in Tim's large hands. He had carried the San Antonio Spurs to a five-game victory over the New York Knicks in the 1999 NBA Finals and now it

Tim wanted to remember this moment with coach Gregg Popovich, so he videotaped it along with the rest of the celebration. (AP/Wide World Photos)

was Tim's turn to carry a video camera. He wanted to record his own story. He was filming the Spurs' celebration on the most famous basketball court in the world, Madison Square Garden in the heart of New York City and he did not want to miss any of the action.

"What people don't know about Tim is that he's a seven-foot kid," explains his best friend on the Spurs, guard Antonio Daniels.

This kid had taken the place of Michael Jordan, who had won six Finals MVP trophies. It took Jordan seven years to win his first championship. Tim won his in only his second season. Winning the MVP award in The Finals, "means the world to me," Tim said. That is because his Spurs became champions.

"Just making records for myself, just keeping it on tape," Duncan said of his camcorder approach. "There's no guarantee I'll ever get back."

He'll be back. You can be sure of that.

In many ways Tim is the best example of the new athletic hero, soft-spoken, bright and team-oriented player. He enjoys the game. He works hard to improve but never lets the weight of the world wear him down. He doesn't take himself or life too seriously. He has a tattoo of Merlin the Magician on his chest and a joker on the back of his right shoulder. Born and raised on St. Croix of the Virgin Islands, he has a relaxed attitude.

Says San Antonio coach Gregg Popovich, "Tim's not an MTV player. He's a basketball player. He's an old-school, work hard, fundamentally sound basketball player."

Tim Duncan is not MTV; he's MVP. After so much "look at me" in the world of sports, the games are going back to the glory of "we."

In baseball there is the smashing success of Mark McGwire, Sammy Sosa and Ken Griffey Jr., three sluggers who have created a new generation of fans with their dramatic home run feats. Several weeks after Tim and the Spurs were victorious, the hearts of America were stolen by the U.S. Women's Soccer team that won the World Cup on Brandi Chastain's penalty kick, setting off an emotional red, white and blue party at the Rose Bowl.

In the NFL, the St. Louis Rams' success story mirrored that of the Spurs. Just as Tim, the young superstar, helped courageous and classy veteran David Robinson win his first NBA title, young running back Terrell Davis helped carry beloved veteran John Elway to back-to-back Super Bowl championships.

Each of these stars have a style all their own. Unlike Jordan, who used to let his tongue and all his talent hang out on the court, Duncan hides be-

Tim keeps his emotions in check on the court. (AP/Wide World Photos)

hind a mask of non-emotion on the floor. Most people don't even know that Tim's tongue is pierced.

"He is a very private person, who doesn't let his jovial, personal side out very often" explained Dave Odom, his coach at Wake Forest.

Tim is a magician on the court and a joker off the floor. "He can be wild and crazy," Daniels says. "On road trips, he busts into my room and if there is a basketball game on, he makes me turn to wrestling. He loves games. He loves toys. We spend a lot of time laughing."

In 1999, Tim and the Spurs got the last laugh. After a 6-8 start, the Spurs were in deep trouble, but the Twin Towers of Tim and David would not collapse. The Spurs would go 46-7 the rest of the way, losing just two games in the playoffs. During the playoff run Tim led the Spurs to an NBA record 12 straight playoff victories.

Tim led the Spurs past the Portland Trailblazers to reach the 1999 NBA Finals. (AP/Wide World Photos)

The Spurs beat Minnesota in the first round, 3-1, then swept past the glitzy Los Angeles Lakers of Kobe Bryant and Shaquille O'Neal, and the Portland Trail Blazers, before toppling the Knicks in five games to win the team's first title in 26 years.

It took only two years for Tim to win a championship. The first time Houston Rockets star Charles Barkley played against Tim he predicted great things, saying, "I have seen the future and he wears No. 21."

Sir Charles was right.

Tim's all-around ability and willingness to pass the basketball is what sets him above the NBA crowd. He is a seven-footer who has the skills of a much smaller player. Even when he shoots there is a form of teamwork in his patented shot—the bank shot. Tim uses the glass to his advantage more than any player in the NBA.

So it was not surprising that in his greatest moment of triumph, Tim was not standing on the Garden floor screaming, "Look at me! Look at what I've done!" Instead, he took a step back and filmed his teammates and their families as they hugged and celebrated on a warm June night. There was 5-10 point guard Avery Johnson, who had hit the game-winning basket, hugging coach Gregg Popovich. Tim recorded three generations of Robinson men celebrating on the floor. Then he went into the locker room where the champagne corks were being popped.

He was directing his own movie after directing the Spurs to a championship. In that final game, it was Latrell Sprewell and Tim who engaged in a shootout, Sprewell scoring 35 points while Tim poured in 31 in the 78-77 victory.

For the series, Tim averaged 27.4 points, 14 rebounds and 2.2 blocks. He was the star and the producer of the championship show. The next day he would continue to record the victory celebration in San Antonio from the moment he stepped off the team plane through the victory parade when the Spurs floated down the city's beautiful River Walk.

Somehow, it was only fitting that he be on the water with the NBA Championship trophy and the Finals MVP trophy in hand for it was in the water that a young Tim Duncan, a championship swimmer, thought his athletic dreams would come true —until a nightmare storm wiped away those dreams in his home in the Virgin Islands.

The dedication Tim learned as a swimmer paid off when he reached the NBA. (AP/Wide World Photos)

CHAPTER TWO

Swimming for Success

Tim grew up in the relaxed atmosphere of St. Croix in the Virgin Islands. The Caribbean island is only 82 square miles and has a population of 56,000.

Basketball was not king when he was a 1993 graduate of St. Dunstan's Episcopal School. Delysia and William Duncan had three children, two girls and a boy. A solid foundation was built. Delysia demanded they get an education and she pushed them into swimming where they would become champions. Swimmers can be the most dedicated of athletes, spending long hours in the pool alone to perfect their skills. It is an individual sport that takes incredible stamina. You alone are responsible for your success or failure. It was where Tim learned to be a champion.

"Swimming did a lot for me training-wise," Tim says, "because it's such an individual training situation where the workout is you get in the water, you do it. You have to find a way."

With that kind of background it is easy to understand why Tim could triumph over tragedy, swim against the tide and find success. The day before his 14th birthday, his mother died of breast cancer.

To this day, though, Delysia lives on in her children. "Her messages," Tim said just before the start of NBA Finals, "are alive forever."

One of those messages is to do your best no matter how difficult the situation. Tim's oldest sister, Cheryl, was a champion swimmer who went on to become a nurse. His other sister, Tricia, excelled in the backstroke and competed in the 1988 Olympics for the Virgin Islands. Tim's specialty was the 400 freestyle, but his grand plans of swimming success changed forever in 1989 because his training pool, the only Olympic-size training pool on the island, was wiped out by the mighty forces of Hurricane Hugo. It was a year later that his mother passed away.

In a first-person article in *Sport Magazine*, Tim wrote of himself, "I've got a million things going on in my head at all times . . . That's why I am a quiet person by nature. After all, it is difficult to think while talking . . . that's why I love being quiet —because I love to think."

He was able to let use sport as an outlet, using all his powers of concentration to succeed. With no pool to train in, Tim had to find another sport to excel so he switched to football and basketball. He did not play his first organized basketball game until the ninth grade. He wasn't much of a fan. "I didn't have much interest in the NBA," he says.

The change did not go smoothly. Tim quickly picked up a nickname: "Mr. Clumsy."

"He used to come over here and play on our court," Nancy Pomroy, the athletic director at Country Day School told the San Antonio Express-News. "He was huge. So big and tall, but he was awfully awkward at the time. Now look at him."

In the end, though, his swimming background made him a better basketball player.

"I came a long way," Tim admits. "But I have a long way to go, too. This wasn't my game. I wasn't born to play. The road took me a different way—I might still be swimming. I'm very fortunate to be where I am today."

In times of trouble on the court he is a player who knows to keep his head above water. He not only outplays opponents, he out-thinks them, too, never letting down his guard on the court. In times of stress, he'll often walk over to veteran teammates and make a joke to relax them. A psychology major at Wake Forest, Tim learned the importance of playing with a clear mind. During one particularly grueling game in his rookie year, he went up to veteran point guard Avery Johnson, who had just blown two layups and asked, "What kind of music do you like to listen to?"

Johnson got the message: Relax. The next season, Johnson would hit the winning basket in the last game of the Finals.

Tim never shows emotion on the court. He may disagree with a referee's call, but only offers a

Tim rarely gets upset on the court, even when an official makes a call with which he disagrees. (AP/Wide World Photos)

few calm words to state his case. The only thing that can be considered emotion is when he sometimes opens his huge "ET" eyes wider than normal. Because he does not show emotion, he has been criticized in the past as not caring enough.

"I try to take this mentally probing attitude on the court with me at all times," he said in his self-analysis. "People in college thought I was lackadaisical because I didn't show emotion. They thought I was soft because I didn't yell with every rebound. Emotions must not always be shown: if you show excitement, then you may also show disappointment or frustration. If your opponent picks up on this frustration, you are at a disadvantage."

It's all part of his Island heritage, where he has been honored in "Tim Duncan Day" ceremonies and has received the island's Medal of Honor, the highest award that can be bestowed upon someone by the territorial government. "I love going back

This mural shows how the people of the Virgin Islands feel about Tim. (AP/Wide World Photos)

home," he said. "It's still a chill place. I don't get stressed a lot at home."

San Antonio coach Gregg Popovich knows exactly the kind of person he has in Tim. Early into his rookie year, his coach explained, "Tim's demeanor is singularly remarkable. "He's on island time. He puts things in perspective, not adding too much importance, not getting too upbeat or too depressed."

And the people of St. Croix are so proud of Tim. "He is a quiet giant," Senate President Vargrave Richards said. "His laid-back attitude is the embodiment of people of St. Croix, doing things without fanfare and hoopla."

With that kind of special makeup, there was no doubt that Tim would be able to leave the island and succeed in college on two fronts—on the basketball court and in the classroom. By getting his degree he would make his mother's dream come true.

Tim excelled in the classroom and on the basketball court at Wake Forest. (AP/Wide World Photos)

3

Growing into the Game

When Tim left for college he was hungry for knowledge. His Wake Forest experience provided a wonderful education for him in so many ways.

In this age of instant gratification when the NBA raids high schools as well as colleges to fill the desperate talent needs of the league, Tim is an exception. He decided to stay in school and is the perfect example of the value of a college education.

He is considered the poster child for staying in school. He loved his time in Winston-Salem, North Carolina and received a degree in psychology. But all his lessons didn't come in the classroom. He grew as a person and a basketball player.

"It helped me to play as a senior," he said of his final year at Wake Forest. "I got stronger, smarter and better prepared."

He then smiled before adding, "Anyway, that's what my mom would've wanted."

His degree is no simple jock degree. As a senior he took courses in psychology, anthropology, Chinese literature and still managed to be the NCAA Player of the Year. He wanted to get the most out of his college experience and he did.

Tim is a deep thinker. He has the ability to take in what is said and how to best use that information. That became clear to Wake Forest coach

Dave Odom when he went to visit Tim in the Virgin Islands on a key recruiting trip. Odom had to rely heavily on the face-to-face portion of this recruiting trip because although Tim averaged 25 points a game and grew to 6-9 his senior year in high school, those numbers came against much less talented teams. Odom had to see what kind of person Tim was, if he had the ability to get better against top-notch competition.

It was Tim's abilities off the court that sold Odom. "His mind works different from most basketball players," Odom once explained to a reporter. "When I visited St. Croix, my pitch didn't seem to be making a dent. I figured he wasn't hearing a word. He just looked at the television. But when I decided to quiz Tim, he had retained everything in great detail. A natural psychologist."

Tim listens and learns. He absorbs information. Deborah Best, the psychology department

A rare display of emotion for Tim during his years at Wake Forest. (AP/Wide World Photos)

chairperson at Wake Forest and Tim's advisor, was impressed with the student, not the basketball player. "Tim hates to hear this," she told the Charlotte Observer during his rookie year in the NBA. "But he was one of my more intellectual students. The best compliment I could give Tim is that other than his height, I couldn't tell him from any other student at Wake Forest."

In his senior year Tim even co-authored a chapter in a psychology reference book. In Tim's typical playful style, the chapter was entitled: "Blowhards, Snobs and Narcissists; Interpersonal Reaction to Excessive Egotism."

His ego was never out of control. He was so stone-faced on the court that Duke fans took to calling him, "Mr. Spock" as in the character from Star Trek. Just as Tim worked on his studies, he continued to work on his game. He used his summers to improve on the court. That hard work paid off in many ways. In his senior year at Wake Forest Tim was the consensus NCAA Player of the Year and the first player to be named a First Team All-American selection by the Associated Press two years in a row since Shaquille O'Neal.

Tim also was named the winner of the coveted Wooden and Naismith Awards. In 31 games he averaged 20.8 points, 14.7 rebounds, which led the nation, and 3.29 blocks in 36.6 minutes a game. He shot .608 from the field. In addition he was the ACC Player of the Year for the second straight season and showed in the ACC tournament a glimpse of the bright future that was ahead when he scored 31 points against Florida and tied a career-high with 33 vs. North Carolina.

This is how far Tim had come. In his first game in college he did not score a point against Division II opponent Alaska-Anchorage. "Tim Duncan,"

Odom says, "was the best listener I ever coached. That mental approach combined with his physical skills is why he is a great player."

When Tim's college career ended in 1997, it was clear that Wake Forest had never seen a player like Tim and probably would never see another one with his all-around ability, height and intelligence. Tim became the first player in NCAA history to finish his career with 1,500 (2,117) points, 1,000 (1,570) rebounds, 400 (481) blocked shots and 200 (288) assists. He blocked at least one shot in 127 of his 128 career games. On Feb. 25, 1997, after his final game at Joel Coliseum, Tim's No. 21 was retired to a standing ovation.

Those 288 assists show how unique he is for his size. Players who are seven foot usually don't have that many assists. Tim's offensive weapons are many—everything from a jump hook to a pivot

*There's a lot more to Tim's game than just monster dunks.
(AP/Wide World Photos)*

and spin to a step-back jumper. One of the basket-ball tools he perfected at Wake Forest was a bank shot. It was that shot that mystified the Knicks in the 1999 Finals, a shot he went to in the critical Game 4 victory. There is irony in the fact that a seven-foot man uses the glass as his best friend. Tim's game is not about the thunder and lightning of the dunk, but of the soft rain of shots like 12-foot bank shots and jumpers. If defenders key on him then he passes to open teammates for the score.

"The bank shot has always been a good shot for me," Tim says. "I've always felt comfortable shooting it. It's just easy for me. It's a lot easier than shooting straight in from that angle. It just feels good."

As for his ball-handling skills, he started as a 6-1 guard in the ninth grade and "Magic (Johnson) was one of my favorite players coming up," he says. "I've always been able to pass. It's something that

Tim celebrated with his father and received a standing ovation as his number was retired at Wake Forest in 1997. (AP/Wide World Photos)

makes the game more fun for me."

Tim is the all-around player and person that he is today because of his experience at Wake Forest. "College did a lot for me," Duncan said during his rookie NBA season. "I would have been much farther behind if I'd come out early."

In school he learned the most valuable of lessons—use all your tools. Then if good fortune happens to pair you with another seven-footer, learn to make the most of that, too.

When Tim moved to Mr. Robinson's neighborhood good things happene
(AP/Wide World Photos)

CHAPTER FOUR

Twin Tower Construction

O ver the last decade San Antonio was Mr. Robinson's Neighborhood. The team and the city belonged to David Robinson since he joined the Spurs in 1989 when he won Rookie of the Year honors. David Robinson truly was the center of attention in every way. He was one of the league's 50 Greatest Players, an MVP winner and an eight-time All-Star. A back injury in 1996-97, though opened the door for Tim to join the team.

Tim shakes hands with NBA commissioner David Stern after the Spurs picked Tim first overall in the 1997 NBA Draft. (AP/Wide World Photos)

In that stormy season the Spurs finished 20-62. They did manage to win their most important contest of the season, though, the NBA Draft Lottery and that is how they were able to draft Tim with the first pick of the 1997 draft.

Tim was the perfect player for the Spurs in many ways. Most importantly, he had ultimate respect for David, a former Naval Academy star, who served in the Navy from June of 1987 until May of 1989. David was both a gentleman and an officer, and that is how Tim treated him.

The same commitment David showed to the Navy and his country he also showed to San Antonio, which made it even more important for Tim to show David respect. Robinson and his wife Valerie established the David Robinson Foundation, which addresses the physical and spiritual needs of the family and in the summer of 1997 David and Valerie donated $5 million to the Carver Complex, a project on the Eastside of San Antonio that will someday include a college prep school as well as community, cultural and arts centers.

Into this world stepped Tim, the perfect first mate for The Admiral.

For Gregg Popovich, who moved from the general manager's office to the coaching sidelines the previous season, the addition of Tim was the silver lining to all the loses in 1996-97. "The only way I can mess him up," Popovich said at the time, "is to coach him too much."

The Texas Towers were born. By the end of Tim's first training camp, Popovich was impressed with his new star. "Man, it's ridiculous how good Tim is," he told reporters. "He can shoot the jumper. He's got range to the three-point line. He's got jump hooks right and left. He can catch it, pull it through and drive it on people." The complete package.

Though Tim had so many skills, he was not afraid to work on his weaknesses, becoming an all-around better player. Tim had used the summer league to improve on his weaknesses, never really showing opponents his "A" game. It takes a special person who has extreme confidence in himself to be willing to work on new things and struggle over a period of time so that he can become a better player down the road. But that is the kind of player Tim is on the floor and the kind of student he was at Wake Forest—study hard and you will be rewarded.

When Tim first arrived in San Antonio, he agreed to participate in the Spurs summer league in Utah and also to work out with David Robinson during the summer so the two big men could make their worlds smaller and get to know one another. It would make the transition of coming into the pros that much easier.

Robinson was impressed with Tim's ability from the start. "He's the real thing," David said. "I'm proud of his attitude and effort. A lot of guys come in and don't want to do anything, but he gives all that extra effort and work and is open to help and wants to become a better player."

The more the two got to know one another, the better friends they became. David became like a big brother to the fellow seven-footer. In Tim he saw himself. "Our personalities are so similar, it's kind of funny," he said. "It's like he's where I was 10 years ago."

During their private workouts together, David put the rookie through the personal test by having him endure the same rigorous schedule even though Tim had just finished playing for the summer league team and was exhausted from that experience.

"I loved being around him," David said of their first extended time together. "I'm really excited about it."

In many ways, successful teams are like successful marriages. There is give and take, and players cannot always think of themselves first. They have to think of how their actions affect their teammates. Instead of being a know-it-all, Tim looked at his bold step into the NBA as a learning process. This is what he told reporters after those early workouts with David. "It was great to see David's training regimen, gain some of the knowledge he's acquired in the years he's been in the league. It helped me set goals and understand what it will take to succeed."

Tim was not just saying those words because he knew that was the right thing to say. He meant every word. Like a student approaching a difficult

All of Tim's hard work was rewarded when he was named NBA Rookie of the Year. (AP/Wide World Photos)

assignment, he now had the perfect outline of success, written personally by one of the NBA's all-time best big men in David Robinson. Tim would have been stupid not to take advantage of the situation.

Watching it all was Popovich. "If Tim throws someone's shot into the 10th row, he's not impressed with himself," Popovich said. "Or if he travels, he doesn't hang his head. He just keeps competing. You can count on 10 fingers the guys you've seen over the years like that."

When the season started, Tim jumped right into the action. In his second-ever road game, Tim hauled down 22 rebounds against Michael Jordan's Bulls and big, bad Dennis Rodman. So much for being the nervous rookie.

Tim went on to have a great rookie year and beat out New Jersey's Keith Van Horn for Rookie of the Year honors, averaging 21.1 points, 11.9 rebounds, 2.7 assists and 2.51 blocks in 39.1 minutes while shooting .549 from the field. The Spurs finished with a 56-26 mark and were knocked out in the second round of the NBA playoffs by the Utah Jazz. The regular season record marked the greatest single-season turnaround in league history as the Spurs won 36 more games than the previous season.

The difference was Tim as he became only the 19th rookie in league history to average 20-plus points and 10-plus rebounds. He became the first rookie since Larry Bird in 1980 to be named to the All-NBA first team. One of the statistics that measures a player's success is his ability to notch double figures in points, rebounds or assists. If you reach two of those categories it is called a double-double. In his rookie year, Tim led the NBA in double-doubles with 57.

Those numbers, though, only tell part of the story. There was more to Tim than hard work and wonderful statistics. There was the other side of this mountain of a man that made the Spurs come together as a team.

Tim is just as happy to pass the ball as he is to shoot it.
(AP/Wide World Photos)

CHAPTER FIVE

Spur of the Moment

Coaches and teammates see a much different Tim Duncan than fans. He is playful, more like a big puppy than an NBA star.

During practice Tim always wears his shorts on backwards, something he started at Wake Forest. It is his way of reminding himself this is all one big game and you have to have fun and not take yourself or your sport too seriously. He has a way of lightening the load for a team during the long hours of practice. He is fun to be around and is not afraid to joke with his teammates.

After Tim's tremendous rookie season, Gregg Popovich told him that he would not overuse him in 1999. Given the news, Tim protested in mock anger, saying, "I thought you were going to expand my game and let me play point guard. Avery Johnson's not that good."

Tim knew that 10-year veteran point guard Avery Johnson, who was once released on Christmas Eve, was standing close enough to hear the kidding remark. Tim loves to joke with his teammates and coaches. That is part of the family atmosphere he brings to the team. And he is not afraid to laugh at himself.

In a *Sport Magazine* article subtitled "The Psychoanalysis of Tim Duncan," that Tim wrote himself he explained personality. "You ever see the movie *Good Will Hunting* starring Matt Damon? If so, you've got a true psychoanalytical picture of me," he wrote. "I'm just a taller, slightly less hyperactive version of the Damon character in the movie. I really enjoyed how he probed people and found out their weaknesses—what they liked and didn't like—just by asking questions and saying outlandish, random stuff just to get a reaction. People expect me to be this shy, quiet type, so I'll ask them outlandish questions in a serious tone."

Ask Tim "Why?" and he's likely to ask, "Why not?"

Tim's ego does not demand the spotlight. He is one of the most down to earth superstars in sports. As his career continues to grow, Tim knows he can seek all the endorsements in the world. He really could Be Like Mike and be a walking advertisement for any product he wanted to endorse. His personality is different, though, and he does not seek that kind of fame.

"That's not me," Tim says quietly. "I'm not that crossover entertainer. I love playing basketball. It comes with the territory, all that stuff. Here and there I'll do some stuff endorsement-wise, but whatever comes. I'm not someone who goes out and has to do a movie this summer or anything like that."

Before a game in the locker room, he can usually be found relaxing in his own unique ways, perhaps kidding with teammates or playing spur of the moment games. Before the start of his first 1999 playoff game, a reporter from *ESPN Magazine* found Tim playing just such a game. Tim tried over and over to drop a plastic sports drink container into a sneaker as good friend Antonio Daniels cheered him on. Away from the court, video games are Tim's passion. In many ways Tim is exactly what he seems to be, a big kid having the time of his life. As he might ask: "Why not?"

Tim is at the top of his profession in just his second season. He has all the toys money can buy, including his Porsche Carrera. He has close friends he can trust and his goal is to lead a stress-free life by working hard for success. For Tim, the joy is in the journey of life.

"I'm not serious most of the time," he says of himself. Most people don't realize that.

"With the media he is kind of standoffish and reserved," Daniels says. "But we hang out all the time and around me he just lets himself go. Don't get fooled by his serious look. There is a little class clown in him."

Tim does not overdo the nightlife scene. What does he do to relax? "We go out to eat a lot," Daniels explains. "We play video games. We go to the arcade sometimes."

On the floor, fans and opponents see a somber Duncan. That is exactly the way he wants it to be—never show too much emotion. "Basketball is like a chess game," he wrote in *Sport Magazine*. "You can't reveal all that you're thinking or you'll be at a siz-

Tim is a very different person away from the basketball court. (AP/Wide World Photos)

able disadvantage to your opponent. Basketball to some players is mainly a physical event. To me, it's both physical and mental. You must not only conquer your opponents physically, you must beat them mentally."

To win the mental battle he has a variety of weapons. When opponents expect a jump shot, he will pump-fake and drive. He can jump hook with either hand. He uses the glass and passes to teammates much more than most big men. But to succeed in his world takes more than talent. It takes a certain strength of character and the ability to come back for situations where you have failed.

Tim showed an inner strength from the start of his NBA career. That is how he won Rookie of the Year honors. Even though the Spurs were ousted in the second round of the playoffs, he showed that inner strength as his first playoffs became a building block for future success.

He made his playoff debut against the Suns. In the fourth quarter of his first playoff game the Spurs went to him seven straight times and seven times they scored. The tone for the series was set as the Spurs eliminated the Suns in four games. Next up was the mighty Utah Jazz.

Tim sprained his left ankle in an overtime loss in Game 2. This followed a one-point loss in the first game when Tim's last-second turnaround jumper hit the back of the rim. On the team bus that night Johnson, the veteran point guard, told the rookie to take the same shot the next time that situation developed in the playoffs.

Tim, who averaged 21 points and 8.4 rebounds in the series, didn't blink and told his point guard, "You better give me the same shot the next time." A key missed shot was not going to dent Tim's confidence.

The Spurs were beaten in five games by the Jazz, who went onto the NBA Finals before losing to Michael Jordan and the Bulls. In defeat, Tim grew as a player. His time was to come the next season and Tim was determined to make the most of that opportunity.

Tim said those first playoffs of his rookie year "were just a start." Coach Gregg Popovich saw it that way, too, saying of Tim, "He's on the road to stardom."

The next time, Tim knew he would make those key shots no matter how difficult the situation. He was poised to become a champion.

Tim's second season would be even better than his rookie year. (AP/Wide World Photos)

CHAPTER SIX

The Road to Glory

The 1998-99 season did not get off to a good start for anyone in the NBA. A labor war between the players and owners delayed the start until February. The first day after the lockout ended, the Spurs held a voluntary practice. Three players showed up. Tim was one of those players. David Robinson was there, too. The big men knew there was no time to waste.

The regular season would last just 91 days. Fifty games played in such a short span of time meant that Tim had to be ready from the start. He knew that the NBA race would be wide open with the retirement of Michael Jordan. He knew the season could belong to the Spurs if the players worked together.

In the chess game that was the 1999 season, it was important for Tim to show his teammates that he was not satisfied with winning Rookie of the Year honors. He had to show them he was about much more than individual goals. Team goals were the prize.

Tim's work ethic was deeply appreciated by his teammates. During the shortened training camp point guard Avery Johnson took note of the bitter way the previous season had ended and of Tim's readiness to start a new season. "Tim worked a little harder in the offseason than I thought he would,"

Johnson told *San Antonio Express-News* columnist Buck Harvey. "I think he really, really wants to get back on the court and make that shot he missed against Utah."

That and more.

Tim was ready for the challenge of replacing Michael. "There's a maturity about him in understanding that he can be the heir apparent in this league," coach Gregg Popovich said. "He understands the responsibility and work ethic that entails."

"This year," David Robinson said with a laugh, "I don't need to tell Tim anything."

In professional sports, though, nothing is handed to you. Tim and the Spurs were tested early. With several key new players on the team the Spurs got off to a slow start. They lost eight of their first 14 games and there was talk Robinson should be traded, breaking up the Texas Towers after just one

The Spurs weathered some early troubles in their championship season. (AP/Wide World Photos)

season. There was also talk that the might make a coaching change. The players, though, stood firmly behind the 50-year-old Popovich, who never played in the NBA but played four seasons at the Air Force Academy and was respected by his players.

The Spurs would weather the early storm and, under Popovich's leadership, Robinson and Duncan became an unstoppable duo.

After that slow start the Spurs put it all together and finished the regular season with a 31-5 run. Tim appeared in all 50 games and averaged 21.7 points, 11.4 rebounds, 2.4 assists and 2.52 blocked shots in 39.3 minutes. For the second straight season he led the league in double-doubles with 37. In the final 36 games, Tim really turned it on, averaging 22.8 points and 11 rebounds, 2.72 blocks, 2.4 assists, 1.06 steals and shooting .512 from the field and .718 from the free-throw line. Every part of his game improved.

At the age of 23, he became the most dominant overall player in the NBA and he had The Admiral alongside to protect him. They became a defensive duo that shut down opponents. The league MVP award would go to the Utah Jazz' Karl Malone even though many felt that Tim deserved the honor. It was no big deal to Tim, though because he had team goals on his mind.

"The thing about Tim is that he is not playing for MVP awards," says his close friend Antonio Daniels. "He's playing for championships."

With Tim leading the way, the Spurs roared through the first two rounds of the playoffs, beating the Minnesota Timberwolves, 3-1, and sweeping the Lakers and Shaquille O'Neal, the player many considered the best center in the NBA. Tim led the Spurs in scoring in that series as he outplayed Shaq, averaging 29 points and 10.7 rebounds while

O'Neal averaged 23.8 points and 13 rebounds. Tim had eight blocks to Shaq's seven and 13 assists while O'Neal only put up two. While Tim shot .809 from the free throw line, O'Neal only shot .475. Tim had shown he was the best big man in the NBA.

The Spurs went on to sweep the Blazers, whose will was broken by Sean Elliott's three-point Memorial Day miracle shot. The Spurs had shocked the NBA world. Even Tim's dad said he was surprised the team had won the West. Most people thought the Jazz would return to the Finals or that the Lakers or Trail Blazers would move to the championship round.

Now, all that was left for the Spurs to do was to beat the New York Knicks, the Cinderella team of the playoffs. It would come down to the Spurs' size against the Knicks' heart. It would come down to the Gotham Guards, Latrell Sprewell and Allan Houston, against the Spurs Twin Towers of Tim and David.

Said Sean Elliott of the matchup, "If we go out and win it, you're going to see a lot of guys who will have their careers fulfilled."

This team of veterans were being led by Tim. "Tim's post game, footwork and fundamentals are picture-perfect," explained Elliott. "It's scary."

The two teams had not met in the regular season because of the conference-based schedule created by the lockout. "They think they're the team of destiny, but so do we," noted Elliott, who played despite serious kidney ailment..

To a man, the Spurs knew they would have to succeed in Madison Square Garden to make their dream come true.

"It's a great place to play," Popovich said of the Garden, which is known as the Mecca of basketball. "It's a place that we all watched a lot of great events, watched basketball when we were all kids."

Ultimately it would be the place where Tim and the Spurs would leave their championship mark.

After the NBA Finals, the Twin Towers took their game overseas for the McDonald's International Championship. (AP/Wide World Photos)

Nice Guys
Finish First

On the cover of the Spurs 1999 playoff guide is a wonderful picture of the Twin Towers. Tim Duncan and David Robinson are standing side-by-side with their backs to the camera. In the end, their mission of winning an NBA championship was accomplished together. As much as Tim helped David, David helped Tim.

"I'd like to think I've helped Tim maybe as much as he's helped me," Robinson wrote in *Sports Illustrated*. "If we lose, the media and the fans don't point fingers at him; they point at me because I'm the veteran. That's a nice deal for him. I wish I'd had it that way when I was younger. Having another high-caliber player on your team makes all the difference. You don't feel so stressed out, like I did early in my career."

Robinson then offered this insight into the burdens and pressures of the professional athlete and why these two towers succeeded where all others failed.

"If Tim goes out and gets 15 points and eight rebounds, that's not the end of the world because I'm capable of picking up the slack. During the eight years before Tim arrived, if I put up those numbers, it was the end of the world—we were going to lose. I love Tim like a brother. He's a precious friend and an awesome talent, but I think my presence frees him up to do his thing."

Tim did just that against the Knicks throughout the Finals, starting with his 33-point performance in Game 1. Tim is nicknamed "The Big Easy" by teammate Mario Elie and he showed why in this game as he effortlessly scored at will. A large group of fans from the Virgin Islands came to the game and they were not disappointed. The Knicks came into the series riding an emotional high from their amazing run in the Eastern Conference, when they became the first eighth-seeded team to win the conference. They relished the role of playing David to the Spurs' Goliath. In that first game, though, Tim made a statement, hitting 13 of his 21 shots, grabbing 16 rebounds and blocking two shots. The Knicks knew they were up against a weapon unlike any they had seen before in these playoffs. Even though the Spurs had 10 days off between series, Tim did not miss a beat.

Tim got off to a great start in Game 1 the finals by hitting
13 of his 21 shots and getting 16 rebounds.
(AP/Wide World Photos)

Knicks coach Jeff Van Gundy could not come up with a way to slow Tim down. "Duncan is the best player in the game," he said. "He's so fundamentally sound. He's not a highlight reel, but a coach's clinic. From a coach's standpoint, that's the beauty."

There was more beauty to behold in Game 2 at the Alamodome as the Knicks were trounced, 80-67. Tim poured in 25 points, grabbed 15 rebounds and blocked four shots. Together the Towers combined for 41 points, 26 rebounds and nine blocked shots. The Knicks starting power forward and center duo of Larry Johnson and Chris Dudley combined for only five points, 12 rebounds and zero blocked shots. It was a mismatch of gigantic proportions.

Tim made the critical play of the game, sneaking in for an offensive rebound on a missed free throw. "Luckily it bounced my way," he said. Luck had nothing to do with it. While the Knicks fell asleep on the line, Tim made the play. He had won the chess game. "I just kind of took off before they could see," he said of the Knick defenders, who were caught flatfooted. At the end of the game, the fans were chanting "Sweep!"

It would not be that easy. In two home games the Spurs had established their dominance, but now the series shifted to New York. The Knicks altered their game-plan and concentrated more on stopping Tim. In the fourth quarter of Game 3 Tim was held scoreless as the Knicks came away with an 89-81 victory. He missed all four of his shots in the final period and committed three turnovers.

Now it was his turn to make an adjustment, pass another test. In Game 4 Tim took command again, scoring 28 points and grabbing a stunning 18 rebounds as the Spurs earned a 96-89 victory.

This time he scored seven points in the fourth quarter. As a result, the Spurs owned a 3-1 lead.

"I wanted to be a lot more effective in the fourth quarter this time around," Tim said after the game. "I knew I didn't play well last game and I just wanted to be effective down there."

Praised Latrell Sprewell, who led the Knicks with 26 points, "Tim has played big all series."

Duncan would never be bigger than Game 5. Like all great athletes, Tim could smell final victory. He did not want the series to go back to San Antonio and give the Knicks any hope of winning the series. "We want to come in very focused this next game and get it out of the way," he said. "We don't want to give them an opportunity for life. We just want to knock them out."

They did with Tim scoring 31 points as Avery Johnson hit the winning basket. In the final seconds, Tim and David smothered Sprewell's last shot

Tim scored 31 points in the fifth and final game of the NBA Finals to earn his Finals MVP award. (AP/Wide World Photos)

to hold onto the 78-77 victory. The Spurs knew Tim was the difference in the series, especially since the Knicks did not have the injured Patrick Ewing. Said Johnson, "To be playing with the best player in the NBA now in Tim is just terrific. He has so much character. I'm honored to be his teammate."

"The thing I love about Tim is that he is never satisfied," Mario Elie added. "He's not your average superstar. He doesn't think he knows it all. He listens."

With that kind of approach, the big numbers will continue. There will be more nights when Tim, championship trophy and camcorder in hand, will record those crowning moments of his career.

The future looks very bright for Tim Duncan.
(AP/Wide World Photos)

Tim Duncan Quick Facts

Full Name: Tim Duncan

Team: San Antonio Spurs

Position: Forward

Number: 21

Height/Weight: 7' 0"/260 lbs.

Birthdate: April 25, 1976

Hometown: St. Croix, Virgin Islands

Years in League: 3

Drafted: 1st overall in 1997

College: Wake Forest University

1999 Highlight: Tim was named the 1999 NBA Finals Most Valuable Player where he averaged 27.4 points, 14.0 rebounds, and 2.2 blocks per game.

Statistical Spotlight: Tim was the first rookie to be named to the All-NBA First Team since Larry Bird in 1980.

Little known fact: Tim Duncan admits to being afraid of heights.

Tim Duncan's NBA Statistics

Career Totals

Year	Games	Min	FG/FGA	FT/FTA	Reb	Blk	Pts
1997-98	82	3204	706/1287	319/482	977	206	1731
1998-99	50	1963	418/845	247/358	571	126	1084
Total	**132**	**5167**	**1124/2132**	**566/840**	**1548**	**332**	**2815**

Career Averages

Year	Games	Min/G	FG %	FT%	RPG	BPG	PPG
1997-98	82	39.1	.549	.662	11.9	2.5	21.1
1998-99	50	39.3	.495	.690	11.4	2.5	21.7
Total	**66.0**	**39.1**	**.527**	**.674**	**11.7**	**2.5**	**21.3**

1999 Double-Doubles Leaders

1.	**Tim Duncan, San Antonio**	**37**
2.	Chris Webber, Sacramento	36
3.	Jason Kidd, Phoenix	30
	Shaquille O'Neal, L.A. Lakers	30
5.	Charles Barkley, Houston	29
	Alonzo Mourning, Miami	29
7.	Antonio McDyess, Denver	28
8.	Dikembe Mutumbo, Atlanta	26
9.	Hakeem Olajuwon, Houston	25
	Kevin Garnett, Minnesota	25

1999 Rebound Leaders

1. Dikembe Mutumbo, Atlanta   610

2. Dan Fortson, Denver   581

3. **Tim Duncan, San Antonio**   **571**

4. Chris Webber, Sacramento   545

5. Antonio McDyess, Denver   537

6. Shaquille O'Neal, L.A. Lakers   525

7. Charles Barkley, Houston   516

8. Alonzo Mourning, Miami   507

9. Vlade Divac, Sacramento   501

10. David Robinson, San Antonio   492

1999 Rebounds per Game Leaders

1.	Dikembe Mutumbo, Atlanta	12.2
2.	Dan Fortson, Denver	11.6
3.	**Tim Duncan, San Antonio**	**11.4**
4.	Alonzo Mourning, Miami	11.0
5.	Antonio McDyess, Denver	10.7
	Shaquille O'Neal, L.A. Lakers	10.7
7.	Kevin Garnett, Minnesota	10.4
8.	David Robinson, San Antonio	10.0
	Vlade Divac, Sacramento	10.0
10.	Brian Grant, Portland	9.8

1999 Field Goals Made per Game Leaders

1.	Shaquille O'Neal, L.A. Lakers	10.4
2.	Allen Iverson, Philadelphia	9.1
3.	Chris Webber, Sacramento	9.0
4.	Kevin Garnett, Minnesota	8.8
5.	**Tim Duncan, San Antonio**	**8.4**
6.	Antonio McDyess, Denver	8.3
7.	Gary Payton, Seattle	8.0
	Karl Malone, Utah	8.0
9.	Juwan Howard, Washington	7.9
10.	Michael Finley, Dallas	7.8

1999 Scoring Leaders

1.	Shaquille O'Neal, L.A. Lakers	1,289
2.	Allen Iverson, Philadelphia	1,284
3.	Karl Malone, Utah	1,164
4.	Shareef Abdur-Rahim, Vancouver	1,152
5.	Gary Payton, Seattle	1,084
	Tim Duncan, San Antonio	**1,084**
7.	Antonio McDyess, Denver	1,061
8.	Grant Hill, Detroit	1,053
9.	Stephon Marbury, New Jersey	1,044
10.	Michael Finley, Dallas	1,009

1999 Blocked Shots Leaders

1.	Alonzo Mourning, Miami	180
2.	Shawn Bradley, Dallas	159
3.	Theo Ratliff, Philadelphia	149
4.	Dikembe Mutumbo, Atlanta	147
5.	Greg Ostertag, Utah	131
6.	**Tim Duncan, San Antonio**	**126**
7.	Hakeem Olajuwon, Houston	123
8.	David Robinson, San Antonio	115
	Antonio McDyess, Denver	115
10.	Patrick Ewing, New York	100

Game by Game in 1999
with Tim Duncan

Date	Opp	W/L	Min	FG/FGA	FT/FTA	Blk	Reb	Pts
2/5	SAC	W	31	9/13	1/3	0	17	19
2/6	MIN	W	37	7/18	8/15	3	14	22
2/8	LAL	L	42	8/24	5/9	1	15	21
2/9	@Min	L	42	2/10	4/10	1	11	8
2/11	@Cle	L	43	15/30	1/2	2	14	31
2/12	@Phi	W	28	6/13	3/4	4	6	15
2/14	@Chi	W	36	4/12	6/10	4	14	14
2/17	PHO	L	41	7/14	6/10	2	12	20
2/19	@LAL	L	39	10/20	6/9	1	11	26
2/21	DET	W	38	6/15	5/6	3	14	17

Date	Opp	W/L	Min	FG/FGA	FT/FTA	Blk	Reb	Pts
2/22	@Min	L	40	4/10	2/2	2	12	10
2/24	SEA	W	39	6/16	6/6	1	13	18
2/26	@Sea	L	39	6/12	10/13	3	9	22
2/28	UTA	L	37	10/17	1/4	1	13	21
3/2	@Hou	W	41	10/23	3/4	5	14	23
3/4	@Dal	W	38	9/16	8/10	1	12	26
3/6	LAC	W	30	10/16	7/7	4	7	27
3/7	@Den	W	46	14/27	6/10	3	13	24
3/10	ORL	W	39	7/15	1/1	1	11	15
3/12	@Pho	W	43	11/21	4/7	2	5	26
3/13	DEN	W	36	10/21	7/9	2	8	27
3/16	@Sac	W	38	13/16	2/9	4	12	29
3/17	@GS	W	37	5/18	7/7	2	17	17
3/19	@Por	L	43	10/17	9/11	5	15	29
3/20	@Van	W	46	9/24	6/7	7	14	24

Date	Opp	W/L	Min	FG/FGA	FT/FTA	Blk	Reb	Pts
3/23	DEN	W	34	9/17	1/2	3	5	19
3/25	@Den	W	33	11/18	6/7	3	6	28
3/26	TOR	L	38	2/7	1/2	3	12	5
3/27	DAL	W	40	9/11	3/7	2	15	21
3/30	SEA	W	42	10/19	6/7	0	9	26
4/1	VAN	W	46	19/31	1/1	6	13	39
4/3	LAC	W	32	5/10	7/10	0	12	17
4/5	GS	W	41	9/18	7/8	5	11	25
4/8	@Hou	W	41	8/16	2/5	1	13	18
4/10	@Pho	L	37	7/14	7/10	3	10	21
4/12	PHO	W	43	11/19	4/5	0	11	26
4/13	@Dal	L	39	9/17	3/6	3	11	21
4/14	MIN	W	32	6/12	4/6	2	10	16
4/16	POR	W	43	5/16	10/15	3	12	20
4/18	HOU	W	45	4/12	3/4	1	9	11

Date	Opp	W/L	Min	FG/FGA	FT/FTA	Blk	Reb	Pts
4/20	@Uta	W	40	15/24	6/8	7	10	36
4/22	DAL	W	32	6/11	2/3	3	10	14
4/24	LAL	W	40	6/11	9/12	3	13	21
4/26	@LAC	W	38	9/16	4/4	3	5	22
4/27	@Sac	L	52	12/28	8/12	0	19	32
4/29	@Van	W	30	7/11	5/7	2	10	19
5/1	POR	W	48	5/14	9/12	2	12	19
5/2	UTA	W	42	10/21	6/10	4	14	26
5/4	@Por	W	43	6/12	1/2	2	6	13
5/5	@GS	W	43	10/22	8/8	1	10	28
Totals		**37-13**	**1,963**	**418/845**	**247/358**	**126**	**571**	**1,084**

Baseball Superstar Series Titles
Collect Them All!

___ Mark McGwire: Mac Attack!

___ #1 *Derek Jeter: The Yankee Kid*

___ #2 *Ken Griffey Jr.: The Home Run Kid*

___ #3 *Randy Johnson: Arizona Heat!*

___ #4 *Sammy Sosa: Slammin' Sammy*

___ #5 *Bernie Williams: Quiet Superstar*

___ #6 *Omar Vizquel: The Man with the Golden Glove*

___ #7 *Mo Vaughn: Angel on a Mission*

___ #8 *Pedro Martinez: Throwing Strikes*

___ #9 *Juan Gonzalez: Juan Gone!*

___ #10 *Tony Gwynn: Mr. Padre*

___ #11 *Kevin Brown: Kevin with a "K"*

___ #12 *Mike Piazza: Mike and the Mets*

___ #13 *Larry Walker: Canadian Rocky*

___ #14 *Nomar Garciaparra: High 5!*

___ #15 *Sandy and Roberto Alomar: Baseball Brothers*

___ #16 *Mark Grace: Winning with Grace*

___ #17 *Curt Schilling: Phillie Phire!*

___ #18 *Alex Rodriguez: A+ Shortstop*

___ #19 *Roger Clemens: Rocket!*

Only $4.95 per book!

Football Superstar Series Titles
Collect Them All!

____ #1 *Ed McCaffrey: Catching a Star*

____ #3 *Peyton Manning: Passing Legacy*

____ #4 *Jake Plummer: Comeback Cardinal*

____ #5 *Mark Brunell: Super Southpaw*

____ #6 *Drew Bledsoe: Patriot Rifle*

____ #7 *Junior Seau: Overcoming the Odds*

____ #8 *Marshall Faulk: Rushing to Glory*

Only $4.95 per book!

**Call Toll Free: 1-877-424-BOOK (2665) or
visit us at www.sportspublishinginc.com**

Basketball Superstar Series Titles
Collect Them All!

____ #1 *Kobe Bryant: The Hollywood Kid*

____ #2 *Keith Van Horn: Nothing But Net*

____ #3 *Antoine Walker: Kentucky Celtic*

____ #4 *Kevin Garnett: Scratching the Surface*

____ #5 *Tim Duncan: Slam Duncan*

____ #6 *Reggie Miller: From Downtown*

____ #7 *Jason Kidd: Rising Sun*

____ #8 *Vince Carter: Air Canada*

Only $4.95 per book!

NASCAR Superstar Series Titles

___ #1 *Jeff Gordon: Rewriting the Record Books*

___ #2 *Dale Jarrett: Son of Thunder*

___ #3 *Dale Earnhardt: The Intimidator*

___ #4 *Tony Stewart: Hottest Thing on Wheels*

Hockey Superstar Series Titles

___ #1 *John LeClair: Flying High*

___ #2 *Mike Richter: Gotham Goalie*

___ #3 *Paul Kariya: Maine Man*

___ #4 *Dominik Hasek: The Dominator*

___ #5 *Jaromir Jagr: Czechmate*

___ #6 *Martin Brodeur: Picture Perfect*

___ #8 *Ray Bourque: Bruins Legend*

Only $4.95 per book!

Collect Them All!